OUR FATHER'S PLAN

STUDY GUIDE

ST. JOHN THE APOSTLE BIBLE STUDY

OUR FATHER'S PLAN

Salvation history from
Genesis to the Catholic Church

STUDY GUIDE

IGNATIUS PRESS   SAN FRANCISCO

This study is based on and intended to be used in conjunction with the EWTN (Eternal Word Television Network) video series *Our Father's Plan* © 1996, distributed by Ignatius Press, P. O. Box 1339, Ft. Collins, CO 80522

Unless otherwise noted, Scripture quotations have been taken from the Revised Standard Version of the Holy Bible, the Old Testament © 1952, the Apocrypha © 1957, the New Testament © 1946, by the Division of Christian Education of the National Council of the Churches of Christ in the United States of America.

Excerpts from the English translation of the *Catechism of the Catholic Church* for the use in the United States of America copyright © 1994, United States Catholic Conference, Inc.—Libreria Editrice Vaticana. English translation of the *Catechism of the Catholic Church: Modifications from the Editio Typica* copyright © 1997, United States Catholic Conference, Inc.—Libreria Editrice Vaticana. Used with permission.

Cover art: *Nativity*, Giovanni Battista Pittone
                    National Gallery, London/SuperStock
Cover design by: Riz Boncan Marsella

ISBN 978-0-89870-940-7
Printed in the United States of America ∞

Due to the revision of the VHS series, as well as the addition of a DVD series, please view the Addendum for lesson breakdowns within the *Our Father's Plan* series. The Addendum is located at http://www.ignatius.com/ofp.pdf

"For I know the plans
I have for you, says the LORD,
plans for welfare and not for evil,
to give you a future
and a hope."

Jeremiah 29:11

ACKNOWLEDGMENT AND THANKS ARE GIVEN TO:

Scott Hahn and Jeff Cavins

For their incredible work within the Church, including their video presentation of *Our Father's Plan* (© 1996 EWTN) on which this study is based and in conjuction with which it is intended to be used.

St. John the Apostle Bible Study Participants

For their hunger and enthusiasm for God's Word, which prompted and fostered the writing of this study.

Fr. Don Buxman

For his support of the St. John's Bible Study, Oregon City, Oregon, through its initial years and for his confidence and encouragement.

Fr. Rich Wallace

For his ongoing support as the study was being written, for his suggestions and advice.

May our work bring glory to *God*.

Providing our inspiration, direction, and perseverance,

the *Holy Spirit* surely had a vital influence on the foundation

of this study. To Him we give thanks and praise.

ABBREVIATIONS

The Old Testament

Gen	Genesis	Song	Song of Solomon
Ex	Exodus	Wis	Wisdom
Lev	Leviticus	Sir	Sirach (Ecclesiasticus)
Num	Numbers	Is	Isaiah
Deut	Deuteronomy	Jer	Jeremiah
Josh	Joshua	Lam	Lamentations
Judg	Judges	Bar	Baruch
Ruth	Ruth	Ezek	Ezekiel
1 Sam	1 Samuel	Dan	Daniel
2 Sam	2 Samuel	Hos	Hosea
1 Kings	1 Kings	Joel	Joel
2 Kings	2 Kings	Amos	Amos
1 Chron	1 Chronicles	Obad	Obadiah
2 Chron	2 Chronicles	Jon	Jonah
Ezra	Ezra	Mic	Micah
Neh	Nehemiah	Nahum	Nahum
Tob	Tobit	Hab	Habakkuk
Jud	Judith	Zeph	Zephaniah
Esther	Esther	Hag	Haggai
Job	Job	Zech	Zechariah
Ps	Psalms	Mal	Malachi
Prov	Proverbs	1 Mac	1 Maccabees
Eccles	Ecclesiastes	2 Mac	2 Maccabees

The New Testament

Mt	Matthew	1 Tim	1 Timothy
Mk	Mark	2 Tim	2 Timothy
Lk	Luke	Tit	Titus
Jn	John	Philem	Philemon
Acts	Acts of the Apostles	Heb	Hebrews
Rom	Romans	Jas	James
1 Cor	1 Corinthians	1 Pet	1 Peter
2 Cor	2 Corinthians	2 Pet	2 Peter
Gal	Galatians	1 Jn	1 John
Eph	Ephesians	2 Jn	2 John
Phil	Philippians	3 Jn	3 John
Col	Colossians	Jude	Jude
1 Thess	1 Thessalonians	Rev	Revelation (Apocalypse)
2 Thess	2 Thessalonians		

SIMPLE KEY TO BIBLE REFERENCES

Gen 1:1	refers to the book of Genesis, chapter 1, verse 1.
Gen 1:1a	refers to the book of Genesis, chapter 1, and the first part of verse 1.
Gen 1:1b	refers to the book of Genesis, chapter 1, and the last part of verse 1.
Gen 1:1–13	refers to the book of Genesis, chapter 1, verses 1 to 13 inclusive.
Gen 1:1–13, 17	refers to the book of Genesis, chapter 1, verses 1 to 13 inclusive and verse 17.
Gen 1:1—3:4	refers to the book of Genesis, chapter 1, verse 1 to chapter 3, verse 4 inclusive.
Gen 1, 3	refers to the book of Genesis, chapters 1 and 3.
Gen 1; 7—10	refers to the book of Genesis, chapter 1 and chapters 7 to 10 inclusive.

INTRODUCTION

What a wonderful gift God has given us in His Word! And yet many of us are not able to make sense of the Bible, to understand the order or significance of events, or what all those laws, rituals, and genealogies mean. Even fewer of us are able to see how the Bible can help us realize the fullness of our faith or give any understanding to why we, as Catholics, do many of the things we do.

Perhaps you have had questions or comments such as these:

- Jesus and the beginning of the Church are in the New Testament, so why do I even need to study the Old Testament? The two seem so different; are they really related?
- If I need to study the Old Testament, how do I make sense of it? It doesn't seem to have a consistent story line and is so confusing.
- I'm more comfortable and familiar with the New Testament but how can I get more out of it for my everyday life? Where is the connection to my Catholic faith: the Sacraments, our devotion to Mary, the priesthood, and our Church's teachings?
- I've tried to read the *Catechism of the Catholic Church* but have not been very successful. Can it be used in my study of the Bible and help me in the understanding and practice of my Catholic faith?

God had a perfect relationship with His children, in the Garden of Eden, but Adam and Eve refused this relationship through their sin, thus separating man from God. From that moment the Father laid out His loving plan for the salavation of His children: Salvation history. God desired to reestablish His relationship with man; in this way He confirmed that He is our Father and we are His children. He will always be faithful and will reveal Himself to us as He guides our way.

This study was developed to be used with the EWTN production of *Our Father's Plan*, consisting of thirteen one-hour segments and presented by Dr. Scott Hahn and Jeff Cavins. By focusing on portions of fourteen books in the Bible, this series gives both a historical and theological overview of salvation history from Genesis to the Catholic Church.

Our Father's Plan can be used for personal as well as group studies. An accompanying Facilitator's Guide provides the intended answers for the more factual biblical and doctrinal questions and thoughtful consideration for the personal application questions. It also includes helpful suggestions for coordinating a Bible study.

Each week's study time is meant to include a final segment, approximately thirty minutes long, for reviewing a portion of the *Our Father's Plan* video or audio tape. Throughout the study this is referred to as the "wrap-up tape segment" and is meant to shed additional clarification or information on that week's lesson. Because this written study of *Our Father's Plan* was developed after the production of the EWTN series, the thirteen one-hour segments needed to be divided. The resulting breaks in the tape are sometimes awkward but strive to divide the content and time factors as best as possible. Information for each week's wrap-up tape segment is given at the end of that week's lesson. The times given are approximate.

In studying a single book of the Bible, the required reading usually flows chapter by chapter. However, in *Our Father's Plan,* the reading is more segmented, being a few verses from one chapter, skipping several other chapters, picking up again a few chapters later with a few more verses and possibly ending in a completely different book. Because of this it is difficult to judge how much reading is actually required for any given week. A way for the participants to anticipate how much reading is actually required for the upcoming lesson is through the "Chapter Equivalent Reading", which is given at the end of each lesson. As an example, look at the end of Lesson 2: "Chapter Equivalent Reading for Lesson 3: 1¼ chapters". This tells you to anticipate that next week's lesson, Lesson 3, will require you to read the equivalent of 1¼ Bible chapters. Chapter Equivalent Reading can be used as an aid in scheduling the time needed to complete the upcoming lesson.

We pray that, with the use of this study, the Bible, the *Catechism of the Catholic Church,* and the *Our Father's Plan* series, others may be touched as these former participants were:

- "What a magnificent and limitless God this study has opened my eyes to."
- "I have been infinitely changed. This study has connected so many things for me and changed my understanding of Catholicism."
- "I am more humble now. This study helped me to see the whole picture, the historical timeline, the progression of events and God's presence."
- "I'm not so overwhelmed by the Bible now. I can flip from one book to another."

INTRODUCTORY WEEK

No reading

There are no study questions for the first week because the first session will be devoted to watching or listening to the entire first tape segment of *Our Father's Plan*. (This segment will last for 55 minutes.) The tape is packed with more theological concepts and information than we will experience in the remainder of the study. It should be considered an overview of *Our Father's Plan* and not an indication of the intensity or depth of the future "wrap-up tape segments".

Notes:

Chapter Equivalent Reading for Lesson 1: 3 chapters

STUDY QUESTIONS

Read Genesis 1:1—4:16

1. The Church has always taught that the Bible is the inspired Word of God. In the *CCC* 104, we are told, "In the sacred books, the Father who is in heaven comes lovingly to meet his children, and talks with them." How might this view of Scripture affect what you hope to gain from this study, Our Father's Plan?

2. The privilege of being able to read the Bible carries with it the responsibility of reading it in truth.

    a) Why is it important to read Scripture in context, in relationship to other writings of the Bible, keeping in mind the author and for whom it was written, and not looking at a single verse on its own? (*CCC* 109–14)

    b) How does the Magisterium of the Catholic Church, the bishops in communion with the Pope, assure truth in our interpretation of Scripture? (*CCC* glossary and *CCC* 85, 95, 113, 120)

3. There are correlations between what was created on days one and four, two and five, and three and six. What are those correlations? (Gen 1:3–28)

4. What does it mean to be created in the image of God? (Gen 1:26–27; *CCC* 355–57, 362–64)

5. If God created all and it was all seen as very good (Gen 1:31), where did evil come from? (*CCC* 2851–52)

6. Anthropomorphism is the attributing of human shape and characteristics to God. Examples of this are found in Genesis. God is said to walk in the Garden (Gen 3:8). In Genesis 2:2–3, He is said to have rested from all the work He had undertaken. Was God tired and in need of rest? Explain. (*CCC* 2172)

7. Read Genesis 3:3–7. God told Adam and Eve they would die if they ate the fruit, while Satan assured them they would not die. Why did Adam and Eve not die after eating the forbidden fruit? (*CCC* 399, 403, 1008, 1018)

8. In Genesis 3:7–10, Adam and Eve hid from God, separated as a result of their sin. Genesis 3:15 brings God's promise of mercy, hope, and victory in Jesus (*CCC* 410). How does this promise continue to be lived out in the Sacrament of Penance (Reconciliation)? (*CCC* 1421–22, 1468)

9. Understanding the sin of Adam and Eve is essential in our own spiritual journey.
   a) In your own words, explain what sin is.
   b) How has your realization of sin been a factor in your journey?
   c) Our culture has inappropriately taken on the role of determining what is good and what is evil. Where do you see this happening?

10. Why did God approve of Abel's offering more than Cain's? (Gen 4:1–8; Heb 11:4, 6; *CCC* 161)

11. In what way are you your brother's keeper? (Gen 4:9–10; Lev 19:18; Mk 12:28–31; Jn 15:12)

The wrap-up tape segment is approximately 23 minutes, ending at a break after Jeff Cavins encourages the reading of chapters 1–11 of Genesis.

Notes:

Notes:

Chapter Equivalent Reading for Lesson 2: ¾ of a chapter

STUDY QUESTIONS

Read Genesis 4:25–26; 6:1–17; 11:1–9

1. What new insight did last week's study give you regarding Genesis 1—4?

2. When have there been situations or times you have found it difficult to accept or believe that God would look at His creation today and find it "very good"? (Gen 1:31)

3. In Genesis 1:28–30, God gave man dominion over creation. How does this imply a moral obligation in our treatment of animals and the environment? (CCC 2415–18)

4. Read Genesis 2:21–24; Matthew 19:4–5; Mark 10:7; 1 Corinthians 7:10–11; Ephesians 5:31–33. How do these readings affect your view of the marriage relationship?

5. Why is it important to pay attention to lineage names (Gen 5:1–32; 10:1–32) when they appear in the Bible?

6. From Adam and Eve, two family lines are followed—the Cain line and the Seth line. The promise of a savior was carried through the Seth line and continued throughout salvation history to the coming of Jesus (Lk 3:23–38). In the Catholic Church, the fullness of truth in the saving grace of Jesus is maintained through what continuing line? (CCC 857, 869)

7. a) Genesis 6:9–10 describes Noah and why he found favor with God. What does it mean to you to "walk with God"?
   b) What are some ways the Church helps us to become stronger and more sure in our "walk with God" and to hear and know God's voice in our lives? (Jn 8:12; 10:3–4; CCC 133, 1131, 2030)

8. a) Why did God send the flood? (Gen 6:5–7)
   b) Which people were on the ark with Noah? (Gen 7:7, 13)

9. a) God gave the rainbow as the sign of the covenant between Himself, Noah, and all the earth. In what way can the appearance of rainbows serve to remind you of God's ongoing covenant?
   b) When clouds appear in your life, how do you allow a little bit of God's light in to create a rainbow? Share an example from your life.

10. **a)** Why did Noah's descendants build the Tower of Babel? (Gen 11:1–4)

    b) What were the consequences? (Gen 11:6–9)

The wrap-up tape segment is 31 minutes. It begins with Dr. Hahn reviewing four themes and ends at the conclusion of Tape 2.

Notes:

Notes:

Chapter Equivalent Reading for Lesson 3: 1¼ chapters

STUDY QUESTIONS

Read Genesis 12:1–9; 15:1–21; 17:1–11

1. What impact did Dr. Hahn's talk last week on covenants have on your understanding of God's faithfulness and the Catholic Church?

2. Based on last week's video, how would you say a contract and covenant differ?

3. God made five covenants with man in the Old Testament. The only time Jesus used the word "covenant" was during the institution of the Eucharist at the Last Supper when He said, ". . . this is my blood of the covenant . . ." (Mt 26:28; Mk 14:24; Lk 22:20). The Latin word for "covenant" or "oath" is *sacramentum*. How does this affect your understanding of the Eucharist and the other Sacraments in the Church? (*CCC* 1150)

4. What three promises did God give Abram? (Gen 15:18, 17:4, 22:18)

5. **a)** Read Genesis 12:1–3 and Acts 7:2–3. Note that it is God who takes the initiative in these readings. In what ways has God taken the initiative in your relationship with Him?
   b) What response does God ask of you, as He did of Abram? (*CCC* 166, 2083)

6. Read Genesis 12:10–13. Are you aware of a time in your life when you or someone close to you was deceitful, cheated, or lied in order to meet selfish needs? How did you feel? What were the results?

7. **a)** In Genesis 14:18, Abram met Melchizedek in Salem. What important biblical city did Salem become? (Ps 76:2; Heb 12:22)
   b) Melchizedek is mentioned in the First Eucharistic Prayer of the Mass. Read Hebrews 7 and *CCC* 58, 1350, and 1544. What is the significance of Melchizedek for the Catholic Church's priesthood?

8. To what was God referring in Genesis 15:13–14 when He spoke to Abram? (Ex 1:7, 10–11; 12:40–41)

9. The covenant ceremony between God and Abram is described in Genesis 15:9–11, 17–21. It involved the splitting of each animal, the placing of each animal half across from the other and *only* God (the flaming torch) passing between the animal halves.

a) What did God's passing between the split animals signify? (Jer 34:18)

b) This was a unilateral covenant with the responsibilities, conditions, and possible consequences being assumed by God Himself. He alone would be subject to the consequences if the covenant was not upheld. Realizing this, how should you view God's faithfulness in your own life?

10. Circumcision was the sign of the covenant between God and His people (Gen 17:11–13).

a) What was circumcision according to the Law? (Gen 17:11–14; *CCC* glossary)

b) Why was Jesus circumcised? (*CCC* 527)

c) What is circumcision in Christ? (Col 2:11–13)

The wrap-up tape segment is 24 minutes, starting at the beginning of Tape 3 and ending with Jeff Cavins finishing his talk and Dr. Hahn beginning.

Notes:

Notes:

Chapter Equivalent Reading for Lesson 4: 2½ chapters

STUDY QUESTIONS

Read Genesis 18:16—19:38; 21:1–7; 22:1–19

1. Saint Paul states that Abraham's faith is a model for Christians (Gal 3:6–9). How does last week's study help you understand this?

2. a) Abraham bargained with the Lord regarding Sodom. What did he ask the Lord? (Gen 18:22–32)
   b) Have you ever bargained with God? What did you learn from that experience?

3. Read Genesis 18:20; 19:13; *CCC* 1867. The sin of the people of Sodom is one of the "sins that cry to heaven". Reflecting on our culture today, what are our "sins that cry to heaven"?

4. Read Genesis 21:1–2. The birth of Isaac teaches us that God's time is not always our time and that God is faithful. When have you had to wait for "God's time"?

5. Typology is a doctrine in which one figure or object prefigures or represents another. Most Scripture scholars see Isaac as prefiguring Christ. Read *CCC* 128–30 and Genesis 22:1–14. Compare the sacrifice of Isaac to that of Jesus.

6. Who were the children of Isaac and Rebekah? (Gen 25:22–26)

7. Who made offerings to God in Genesis? (Gen 4:4; 8:20; 12:8; 26:25; 28:18)

8. What offerings are made to God during Mass? (*CCC* 1333, 1350–51, 1368)

9. Read *CCC* 345–48 and 2184–88. The Sabbath is referred to as a day God blessed and made holy, a day of grace and rest from work (Gen 2:3).
   a) Why is the Sabbath blessed and holy? (Ex 20:11; *CCC* 345–48)
   b) How do or should you observe the Lord's Day and keep it holy? (*CCC* 2172–73, 2193–94)

10. Read Revelation 12:3, 9. Many of us have seen pictures showing a snake tempting Adam and Eve. In Genesis 3:1, the Hebrew word *nahash* can

mean "snake", but it can also mean "serpent" or "dragon". This is the same Hebrew word used in Revelation. How could this image change your way of picturing the scene between Adam, Eve, and the "snake"?

11. A temptation may be involved when you find yourself doubting the truth. (Gen 3:1; 1 Pet 5:8)
    a) Have there been half-truths that you acted upon that you wish you had not?
    b) What do you do to strengthen yourself against the deception of the evil one?

The wrap-up tape segment is 30 minutes, starting with Dr. Hahn reviewing Genesis 1 and ending at the conclusion of Tape 3.

Notes:

Notes:

Chapter Equivalent Reading for Lesson 5: 5 chapters

STUDY QUESTIONS

Read Genesis 27:1–46; 32:23–32; 37:3–36; 39:7–23;
41:1–14, 25–40; 42:1–9; 45:1–15; 47:27–48:21

1. God continues to make man in His image and likeness. When do you most reflect the image of God?

2. Blessings are evident throughout salvation history. In the Catholic Church, we are blessed by our priests and encouraged to bless our children. What does it mean for us to bless God? (1 Chron 29:10–20; Ps 34:1; 103:1–2; *CCC* 2626, 2644–45)

3. The blessing included in the first-born son's birthright prayed for fertility, monetary inheritance, and the power to rule his family and others. It was communicated from the father's strength and authority. Once spoken, the blessing could not be recalled.
   a) Did Esau value his birthright? Why or why not? (Gen 25:29–34)
   b) Who received the blessing from Isaac? (Gen 27:27–29)
   c) As a follower of Christ, what is your birthright? (Jn 1:12; 2 Cor 5:17; Gal 4:5–7; 2 Pet 1:4; *CCC* 1996) How do you value it?

4. Spiritual writers have seen the story of Jacob wrestling with an angel as an image of spiritual battles. The most fundamental of these struggles is conversion of heart.
   a) What does "conversion of heart" mean? (*CCC* 1430–32, 2608–9)
   b) What are you wrestling with in your ongoing conversion?

5. God changed the names of Abram (Gen 17:5), Sarai (Gen 17:15), and Jacob (Gen 32:28).
   a) What significance is there to these name changes?
   b) What are examples of name changes in the New Testament or in current Church practices? (Mt 16:17–18)

6. a) List the names of the twelve sons of Jacob (Gen 35:23-26).
   b) What is their significance? (Gen 49:28)

7. a) What did Joseph dream about in Genesis 37:6–10?
   b) Why did these dreams alienate his brothers?
   c) How did Joseph's dreams come to pass? (Gen 42:6–8)

8. Joseph endured many trials in his life, seeing them as part of God's providence.
   a) How is God's hand evident in the sale of Joseph to the Ishmaelites and his resulting years in Egypt? (Gen 45:7–8; 50:20)
   b) Recall a trial in your life where, in the end, you could see God's providence.

9. In Genesis 49 we read Jacob's dying words to his sons. How do verses 8–9 relate to Hebrews 7:13–14, Revelation 5:5, and 22:16?

10. Another evidence of typology (lesson 4, question 5) is seen in the comparison of Joseph's life to that of Christ. List some similarities that make Joseph a Christ-figure. (Gen 37:14 and Mt 1:21b; Gen 37:18 and Mt 26:24–25; Gen 37:28 and Mt 26:14–16; Gen 41:46 and Lk 3:23)

The wrap-up tape segment is 29 minutes, starting at the beginning of Tape 4 and the reading of Jeremiah 29:11. It ends with Jeff Cavins' talk and encouragement to read Exodus.

Notes:

Notes:

Chapter Equivalent Reading for Lesson 6: 10¾ chapters

STUDY QUESTIONS

Read Ex 1:1—12:51

1. We have completed our reading of Genesis, the story of the beginnings of the relationship between God and man. God's plan unfolded despite the waywardness of the people, and God continually drew them back. Share the beginnings of your own faith journey. How do you fit into Our Father's Plan?

2. After the death of Joseph, a new king came into power. This king did not know Joseph (Ex 1:8), meaning that he had no bond with Joseph and he ignored the services that Joseph had rendered to Egypt.
   a) What were the consequences to the Israelites? (Ex 1:11–16)
   b) The child Moses, whom the Egyptians would have put to death, was instead raised with great dignity in Pharaoh's own court with all the benefits given to one of his sons. What was guiding these seemingly impossible events? (*CCC* 302, 303, 306)

3. a) What does the name Moses mean? (Ex 2:10)
   b) Why did Pharaoh's daughter choose that name?

4. Although adopted by Pharaoh's daughter, Moses felt a kinship with the Hebrews (Ex 2:7–10). As a young man, he saw how poorly the sons of Israel were treated.
   a) What was Moses' response when he saw an Egyptian strike a Hebrew? (Ex 2:11–12)
   b) Why was Moses forced to flee to Midian? (Ex 2:15)

5. The revelation of the divine name to Moses (Ex 3:14) is significant because, throughout salvation history, it will be the name used to invoke God. What does God's divine name reveal about Himself? (*CCC* 206–7; Jn 13:19; 18:5–8)

6. Concerning Moses' exchange with the Lord (Ex 3), it has been said, "Moses' conversation with the Lord is a beautiful prayer and one worth imitating. By following his example, a Christian can dialogue personally and intimately with the Lord" (*The Navarre Bible: The Pentateuch*, p. 257).
   a) What is prayer? (*CCC* 2558–61, and glossary)
   b) Where does prayer come from? (*CCC* 2562–64)

c) What can you share about your prayer life?

7. In Exodus 3:11; 6:28–30, it is evident that Moses felt he was unqualified for the task God called him to do. When have you felt, as Moses did, that God asked you to do something that seemed beyond your abilities?

8. "Hardness of heart" is not limited to Pharaoh's dealings with Moses.
   a) What are some other incidences of "hardness of heart" mentioned in the Bible? (Mt 19:8; Mk 3:3–5; 16:14)
   b) What are some consequences of "hardness of heart" for the Christian today? (*CCC* 368, 1859, 1864, 2840)

9. The magicians of Pharaoh were able to "match", through sorcery, the three signs that God gave Moses and Aaron. What does the Church teach about things like horoscopes, astrology, Ouija boards, and fortune-tellers? (*CCC* 2116–17; Deut 18:10–12)

10. Egyptians worshipped snakes, the Nile, frogs, and other creatures as though they were gods. What were the plagues God sent on Egypt? (Ex 7:19—11:5; 12:29)

11. The Passover took place the night before Moses and the Israelites left Egypt.
   a) What is the meaning of the word "Passover"? (Ex 12:13; *CCC* glossary)
   b) What rules were prescribed for the Passover ritual? (Ex 12:1–12, 46)

12. Remembering and celebrating are important in human existence. The Jewish religion places great importance on the annual celebration, the memorial, of the Passover—the event that gave them their life and freedom.
   a) What is the special word for the "memorial" we celebrate in the Eucharistic Prayers? (*CCC* 1354, 1362, and glossary)
   b) What are we commemorating, and why is it important to celebrate? (*CCC* 1341, 1363–64; 1 Cor 10:16; 11:23–25)

The wrap-up tape segment is 22 minutes. It begins with Dr. Hahn's and Jeff Cavins' discussion of Exodus and ends at the conclusion of Tape 4.

Notes:

_____

_____

_____

Notes:

19

Notes:

Chapter Equivalent Reading for Lesson 7: 10½ chapters

STUDY QUESTIONS

Read Exodus 12:33—14:31; 19–20; 23:14—25:16; 28;
30:1–10, 22-30; 31:18—34:35

1. In Exodus 4:22 God declared "Israel is my first-born son." In saying that, God revealed His Fatherhood.
   a) How did Pharaoh's and God's treatment of their first-born differ? (Ex 11:5, 9; 12:23; Hos 11:1–4)
   b) What does it mean that God is Father? (*CCC* 238–40)

2. When the Israelites departed Egypt, why did God lead them through the wilderness instead of taking the more direct route through the land occupied by the Philistines? (Ex 13:17–18)

3. What was the purpose of the cloud that was present by day and the fire that was present by night? (Ex 13:21–22)

4. a) Exodus 15:3 reveals "The Lord is a man of war. . . ." God, displaying His power and sovereignty, is awesome to observe. Describe when you have seen God's power at work.
   b) Read *CCC* 2586–87; Psalm 66:5–6. Write your own hymn of praise to God.

5. How do the following events relate to Christianity today: the infant Moses being removed from the water (Ex 2:5–10), the Israelites crossing the Red Sea (Ex 14:21–22), the water flowing from the rock (Ex 17:1–7), and the water flowing from the side of Christ (Jn 19:34)? (Jn 4:10–14; 7:38; 19:34; 1 Cor 10:2,4; Rev 22:17; *CCC* 117, no. 1, 694, 1094, 1221)

6. God gave the Israelites "bread from heaven" to nourish them during their wandering in the desert (Ex 16:4–35).
   a) What was this "bread from heaven" called, and what did it prefigure? (*CCC* 1094)
   b) Why were the Israelites instructed not to save the "bread from heaven" for the following day? (Ex 16:4, 12, 19)
   c) What is the daily bread God gives us in the Church today? (*CCC* 2837, 2861; Mt 6:11)

7. God selected the nation of Israel for three roles listed in Exodus 19:5–6 and 1 Peter 2:9. Name those three roles.

8. A theophany is a revelation or visible appearance of God, which reveals Him as perfectly and absolutely above man and nature. Read Hebrews 12:18–29, in which Paul compares the Sinai theophany (Ex 19:16–19) to that of the New Covenant.

    a) What response are we to have to a theophany? (Heb 12:28)

    b) Outwardly, how do (or should) we show reverence when coming into God's presence?

9. God gave the Israelites the Ten Commandments (Ex 20:1–17). These commandments were written on two tablets, which may be viewed as an indication of the natural "division" between the first three and the other seven commandments.

    a) In the Old Testament, what do the first three and the last seven commandments concern? (*CCC* 2067)

    b) In the New Testament, how is this "division" seen in the teachings of Christ? (Mt 22:35–40; *CCC* 2055)

10. Why is the Law (the Ten Commandments) called a gift? (Mt 11:30; *CCC* 2059–62)

11. **a)** In the incident of the golden calf (Ex 32:1–35) what did Aaron and the people do while Moses was up on the mountain?

    b) How did Moses react?

    c) How did the Levites respond to Moses' call, and how did this affect their position? (Ex 4:14; 32:25–29; Num 1:50–54)

12. Moses had been on the mountain with the Lord for a short amount of time when the Israelites fell into idolatry (Ex 32:1). How easily we can do the same. What are some things you can do to make sure you put God first in your life?

The wrap-up tape segment is 24 minutes. It starts at the beginning of Tape 5 and ends abruptly with Dr. Hahn's explanation of Numbers 25, the line of Phineus and the mention of the institution of the Covenant of Deuteronomy.

Notes:

_____

_____

_____

_____

_____

Notes:

Chapter Equivalent Reading for Lesson 8: 15 chapters

Read Numbers 13; 14; 17:16–28; 18; 20–25;
Deuteronomy 28:69; 29–34

1. In reading Exodus, what touched you most about God's Divine Providence in leading His people out of Egypt?

2. **a)** How many men were sent out as spies from the wilderness of Paran at Kadesh? (Num 13:2)
   b) How many days were spent spying? (Num 13:25)
   c) What were the two reports given to Moses? (Num 13:27–33: 14:6–8)

3. **a)** Why were the Israelites not successful in their first attempt to enter Canaan, the Promised Land? (Num 14:9–10, 41–45)
   b) Why did the Israelites wander for forty years? (Num 14:33–35)

4. Because of their faith and trust in the Lord, Joshua and Caleb were allowed to enter the Promised Land. What does this tell you about what your own response to God should be?

5. **a)** What two distinctions are made in the Old Testament regarding the ways a person can sin against the commandments that the Lord gave to Moses? (Num 15:22–31)
   b) What are the two distinctions the Church makes concerning sins? (Heb 10:26; 1 Jn 5:16–17; *CCC* 1854–56)
   c) What is the effect of venial sin? (*CCC* 1862–63)
   d) What are the three conditions necessary for sin to be mortal? (*CCC* 1857–60)

6. Punishments that were experienced by some of the Israelites seem harsh (Ex 32:27–28; Num 16:28–33; 25:1–9). To rebel against the order established by God was a serious matter, and God dealt swiftly and definitively with those who did so. What can we expect if we choose to rebel against God? (*CCC* 1022, 1037–39)

7. What was the sin Moses and the people committed at the waters of Meribah? (Num 20:7–13; Ps 95:8–10; Heb 3:15–16)

8. God commanded Moses to make a bronze serpent and mount it on a pole. Anyone who had been bitten by the fiery serpent but looked upon the bronze serpent would be healed (Num 21:4–9).

a) How is the bronze serpent a type (lesson 4, question 5, and *CCC* 128) of the salvation process? (Num 21:9; Jn 3:14)

b) God had explicitly forbidden the making of "graven images" (Deut 4:15–16). How does the Church justify the use of images (crucifixes, statues, icons, and so forth)? (*CCC* 2130–32)

9. Balaam was hired by the prince of Moab to curse the Israelites (Num 22—24). Because of the Lord (Yahweh), what happened to the curses? (Num 23:11–12, 25-26; 24:10–13)

10. The covenant that God made with the first generation at Sinai differs from the covenant made at Moab, forty years later, the Deuteronomic Covenant. Saint Thomas said that a wise and prudent law giver assesses the condition of the people, so as not to set a standard so high it is unobtainable. Some of the provisions of the Deuteronomic Covenant tolerated a lesser evil in order to avoid a greater one.

a) God made the covenant with the people at Sinai. Whom did God direct to make the covenant with the people at Moab? (Deut 27:1; 29:1)

b) Why was divorce allowed in the Deuteronomic Covenant (Deut 24:1–4)? (Mt 19:3–9; Mk 10:2–12; *CCC* 1610)

11. Deuteronomy is oratorical in style; it consists of three sermons by Moses to the people. Deuteronomy 29:1–29 is Moses' third sermon. What is his final summation of the choice facing Israel? (Deut 29:17; 30:15–20)

The wrap-up tape segment is 28 minutes. It starts with Jeff Cavins asking Dr. Hahn where and how the book of Deuteronomy fits into the Pentateuch, and it ends at the conclusion of Tape 5.

Notes:

Notes:

Chapter Equivalent Reading for Lesson 9: 11¼ chapters

Read Joshua 1–6; 13:7—19:51; 23

1. The book of Joshua tells how the Israelites settled in Canaan, showing God's faithfulness to His covenant with Abram in Genesis 12:1–3. How are you seeing Our Father's Plan unfold?

2. Read Joshua 2:1–24. Rahab was a prostitute, looked down on by society, a foreigner or outsider in comparison with God's Chosen People, Israel. In spite of her background and position in society, she chose to help the spies of Israel.
   a) For what would Rahab be remembered? (Heb 11:31; Jas 2:24–26)
   b) As a member of the Church family, what does your faith lead you to do?
   c) Rahab is mentioned in the genealogy given by Matthew (chapter 1). Name some of her descendants. Who is the last descendant? (Mt 1:5, 16)

3. a) As the Israelites were preparing to cross the Jordan into Canaan, what were they told to follow so they would know the correct path to take? (Josh 3:1–5)
   b) How are you to know which path to take in life? (*CCC* 1696, 1698)

4. On entering the Promised Land, God gave the Israelites very specific instructions for the deliverance of Jericho. There were several truths that God wanted them to realize:
   • The battle was God's, and He was with them.
   • Victory was not to be won by military means but by supernatural means.
   • Their strength was in their priesthood.
   a) Which tribe was to lead the Israelites around the city wall, and what were they to carry? (Josh 6:6; *CCC* 1539)
   b) How do you think the Israelites might have viewed the Levites after the fall of Jericho?

5. In Achan's failure to observe the ban, harsh punishment was brought upon him and all of the Israelites (Josh 7).
   a) What was the ban? (Josh 6:18–19, 21)
   b) What was the reason for the ban?

6. Why is it difficult to be patient and obedient, trusting God to work in our lives on His terms?

7. Joshua's conquest of the Promised Land is an allegory of Jesus' spiritual conquest of the whole world. As a member of the Church, the Mystical Body of Christ, what is your role in the "spiritual conquest" of the world? (*CCC* 739, 900)

8. The Israelites had initially been designated by God to be "a kingdom of priests and a holy nation" (Ex 19:6). However, after the golden calf (Ex 32:1–35), because the Levites had been "for the Lord", only their tribe served as priests. As priests, when they entered the Promised Land, the Levites were not given a division of the land as were the other tribes; their heritage was the Lord (Josh 13:14; 18:7). As Catholics our heritage is also the Lord, Jesus Christ. We are sacramentally born into His family.
   a) How is it that we, in the Church, are a "kingdom of priests"? (1 Pet 2:5, 9; Rev 1:5–6; *CCC* 784)
   b) Name the three types of priesthood in the Church. (Heb 4:14; *CCC* 1546–47, 1591–92)

9. Mt. Ebal was north of Mt. Gerizim. Between the two mountains was the city of Shechem. With its central position, it was suitable for tribal gatherings.
   a) What other significance does Shechem have in the Old Testament? (Gen 12:6–7; 33:18–20; 35:2–4; Deut 27:4, 11–14; Josh 8:30–35; 24:1, 25, 32)
   b) What significance does it have in the New Testament? (Jn 4:4–6)

10. The Promised Land was divided into twelve parts. Joseph's two sons' descendants each received one, and the others were given to ten tribes. The Levites did not receive designated land but lived among the other tribes. The more "choice" the land, the smaller was the land size. Using the key below, fill in each land area of the map on page 77 with the correct tribe's name.

A – Asher	E – Gad	I – Naphtali
B – Benjamin	F – Issachar	J – Reuben
C – Dan	G – Judah	K – Simeon
D – Ephraim	H – Manasseh	L - Zebulun

11. Read Joshua 23:1–16. In this passage we see that the Lord had been completely faithful in all He promised to do for the Israelites. Joshua exhorted the people to be totally faithful to the Lord and *all* His Laws. The term "cafeteria Catholic" has been used to describe Catholics who pick and choose which teachings of the Church they will follow. Can

Catholics choose which teachings to follow and still be in complete union with the Church? (*CCC* 837, 891–92)

The wrap-up tape segment is 28 minutes. It starts at the beginning of Tape 6 and ends abruptly with Jeff Cavins' statement that we'll be talking about the book of Judges in just a minute and that there is a corruption among the Levites.

Notes:

Notes:

Chapter Equivalent Reading for Lesson 10: 15¼ chapters

Read Judges 1:1—2:23; 4–16

1. What new insights did you gain from last week's study and/or video?

2. The Israelites were able to inherit the Promised Land under the spiritual and military leadership of Joshua, a leader who was steadfast in the Lord and whose knowledge of the Lord was able to keep the people faithful to Him. After the death of Joshua, the absence of a leader who knew God plunged the Israelites into a faith crisis. What happened when they had no spiritual leader and "every man did what was right in his own eyes" (Judg 17:6; 21:25)? (Judg 3:7–8, 12–13; 4:1–2)

3. Among many other tasks, one of the responsibilities of the judges of Israel was to lead the people to a knowledge of God, to ensure that the people did not act simply on the basis of what *they* thought was right but that they correctly obeyed the commandments and statutes of God. The judges' authority and power were the result of the Lord's Spirit being upon them. Compare this aspect of the judges' duties to the Magisterium of the Catholic Church. (*CCC* 85–87, 890)

4. Samson's mother received instructions from an angel to raise her son differently than she ordinarily would have (Judg 13:5, 8, 12).
   a) What was the Nazarite vow? (Num 6:2–8)
   b) How should you live differently because you are a Christian?

5. When have you experienced a unique time of usefulness to God as Deborah did? (Judg 4:4–5:31)

6. The Book of Judges emphasized what happened to the People of God when they were without a leader who was steadfast in the Lord. Lacking a leader, the Israelites fell into a five-point sin cycle (Josh 3:7–11):

Sin (They displeased God.)
Servitude (They fell under the power of another.)
Supplication (They cried out to the Lord—prayer.)
Salvation (A judge was raised up to deliver them.)
Silence (They were at peace.)

The Book of Judges records that the Israelites repeated this sin cycle seven times. Read Judges 3:7, 12; 4:1; 6:1; 10:6; 13:1. In all of these passages, the Israelites offended God. How do we as Catholics seek reconciliation for the times when we have offended the Lord? (Jn 20:23; Jas 5:16; CCC 1422, 1424)

7. The influence of idolatry from the surrounding people was a constant problem for the Israelites (Judg 10:6–7).
   a) What distinguished the pagan gods from the One, True God? (Ps 115:4–8; *CCC* 2085–86, 2112)
   b) It is a continual, ongoing battle for each individual to recognize and to reject the "gods" of the secular world. How are we to understand idolatry? (Mk 6:24; 12:28–30; *CCC* 2113–14, 2135–36)

8. Our society is very similar to the societies of old. The Israelites had trouble keeping the goodness of God fresh in their minds. Read Judges 8:33–35. What can or do you do to keep the awareness of how much God loves you and does for you fresh in your mind and heart?

9. Read Judges 6:11–24; 13:2–21. Throughout salvation history, God has sent His angels to intervene in human events and to be the carriers of heavenly messages. Angels closed the Garden of Eden, protected Lot, saved Hagar and Ishmael, stopped Abraham's sacrificing of Isaac, announced coming births, and so forth.
   a) What are some truths concerning angels? (Mt 18:10; Heb 1:14; *CCC* 328–30, 334–36)
   b) How has your belief in the presence of God's angels influenced your life?

The wrap-up tape segment is 25 minutes, starting with Jeff Cavins' reading of Joshua 24:15 and ending at the conclusion of Tape 6.
Note: Please review question 8 of next week's lesson early in the week.

Notes:

Chapter Equivalent Reading for Lesson 11: 6¾ chapters

STUDY QUESTIONS

Read 1 Samuel 1:1–20; 7—10; 16—17

1. What was most meaningful for you from last week's study?

2. Hannah was barren until God blessed her with her son, Samuel. What other figures in the Old and New Testaments were born of barren women? (Gen 16:1a; 21:2–3; 25:21, 25–26; 30:22–24; Judg 13:2, 24; Lk 1:7, 57, 60)

3. Read 1 Samuel 2:1–10. Hannah prayed this canticle when she presented Samuel to the Lord. How is this like Mary's Magnificat? (Lk 1:46–55; *CCC* 2619)

4. God is continually speaking in our world. His voice is not always heard. How do you listen to God? (1 Sam 3:9; Ps 119: 27, 169–176; *CCC* 1777)

5. a) The Israelites wanted a king to rule over them like other nations. What did God tell Samuel would happen to the people under the rule of a king? (1 Sam 8:10–18)

    b) God knew that, in their persistence, the Israelites were actually refusing Him as their King. There may be times when you think you know what is best for your future or desire what others have. What should be your desire? (CCC 2541, 2544, 2548)

6. Anointing with oil was a very common practice during biblical times.
    a) What were the reasons for the anointings that took place in 1 Samuel 10:1 and 16:12–13?
    b) How is the title "Anointed One" perfect for Christ's Divine Mission? (Lk 4:16–21; *CCC* 436, 438)
    c) What are the effects of anointings done in the Church today? (*CCC* 1293–94; 2 Cor 2:15–16)

7. How was David like Joseph with regard to his brothers? (Gen 37; 1 Sam 17:14–28)

8. In the Church we are called to priesthood, a call not only to be holy, but also to be a blessing (*CCC* 1669). This week, if possible, you are asked to lay hands physically on someone else—a child, spouse, mother, father, neighbor, or friend—and ask for God's blessing on that person. Share your experience with your group.

9. The story of Samuel connects persons of significant stature—Samuel, Saul, and David. However, it is only with a seemingly insignificant person, Hannah, that it all began. Share a time when you seemed to have little power or knowledge yet you accomplished something of significance. (1 Sam 1; 1 Cor 2:4; *CCC* 489)

10. Goliath was a huge Philistine soldier, an experienced champion, well-equipped with armor and weapons (1 Sam 17:4–7). David was a young, ill-equipped shepherd. David fought Goliath because Goliath had presumed to ". . . defy the armies of the living God" (1 Sam 17:26), which was the same as insulting the God of Israel. Read 1 Samuel 17:37. How could David be so certain that the Lord would keep him safe? (*CCC* 222, 227; 2 Sam 22:2–3; 1 Chron 5:20)

The wrap-up tape segment is 24 minutes, starting at the beginning of Tape 7 and ending with Dr. Hahn's reminder that the God we worship, love, and serve is faithful and keeps His promises.

Note: Please review question 1 of next week's lesson early in the week.

Notes:

Notes:

Chapter Equivalent Reading for Lesson 12: 6¼ chapters

STUDY QUESTIONS

Read 2 Samuel 1:1—5:25; 11:1—12:24

1. Last week we heard Hannah's beautiful canticle (1 Sam 2:1–10) as we learned how she presented Samuel to the Lord. We also saw its similarities to Mary's Magnificat, which Mary prayed when she visited Elizabeth. This song expressed Mary's rejoicing in God's goodness and blessings. This week, take time each day to read the Magnificat (Lk 1:46–55), prayerfully reflecting on God's presence, goodness, and blessings in your life. How were you affected by this daily prayer and reflection?

2. a) In 1 and 2 Samuel, David was anointed three times. In what cities was David anointed and by whom? (1 Sam 16:4, 12–13; 2 Sam 2:1, 4; 2 Sam 5:1–3)
   b) In which cities did David reign? (2 Sam 5:4–5)

3. For all the years after its construction, the Ark of the Lord had dwelled in a tent. David, being given ". . . rest from all his enemies round about . . .", now wanted to build a house of cedar in which the Ark might dwell (2 Sam 7:1–2).
   a) Why did David think this was the time to build a dwelling place for the Ark? (Deut 12:4–5, 10, 13, 14)
   b) What was God's response to David? (2 Sam 7:5–7, 12–13)
   c) In the Catholic Church, what do we call the special house where the Lord dwells? (*CCC* 1379)

4. What does God promise in His covenant with David? (2 Sam 7:15–16)

5. We have learned that one of the responsibilities of the judges was to ensure that the commandments and statutes of God were correctly obeyed. Dr. Hahn refers to Samuel as the thirteenth judge and a prophet. What were prophets? (*CCC* 64, 2581, 2595)

6. Nathan was one of the prophets of the Old Testament. David's reply to Nathan's oracle in 2 Samuel 7:18–29 displays true humility. Read 1 Corinthians 4:7.
   a) Based on these passages, define humility in your own words.
   b) What is the importance of humility in the Christian life? (*CCC* 2559)

7. While staying in Jerusalem, instead of leading his soldiers in battle,

David sinned against God with Bathsheba (2 Sam 11). Second Samuel 11:27 reads, "But the thing that David had done displeased the Lord."

a) What was the sin that started David's downward spiral of sinning? (*CCC* 2538)

b) What other sins can be "born" of this sin? (Gen 4:3–8; 1 Kings 21:1–29; *CCC* 2539)

c) What can often be the source of this sin? (*CCC* 2540)

8. a) What were the consequences of David's sin? (2 Sam 12:13–14)

   b) After Bathsheba married David, she bore him a second son. What was his name? (2 Sam 12:24)

9. In looking at Israel's first two kings, we can see that initially God gave the Israelites Saul, a man with a heart like theirs. Then they were given David, a man after God's own heart (Acts 13:22).

a) What does it mean to be a person after God's own heart? (*CCC* 2579)

b) Many of the psalms are attributed to David. Share one of your favorite psalms.

The wrap-up tape segment is 30 minutes, starting with the continuation of Dr. Hahn's and Jeff Cavins' discussion, going back into 1 Samuel, and ending at the conclusion of Tape 7.

Notes:

Chapter Equivalent Reading for Lesson 13: 17 ¼ chapters

STUDY QUESTIONS

Read 1 Kings 1:28—2:12; 5:1—8:66; 11:1—12:20;
14:21–31; 16:29—22:40

1. Last week as we were learning more about David, what most impressed you—considering both his strengths and his weaknesses—about one of the following: his relationship with God, his kingship, or his humanness?

2. King David called Bathsheba to come before him. He swore an oath that her son, Solomon, would be the next king. How does Solomon's arrival at the city prefigure Jesus and His arrival? (1 Kings 1:33–34; Mt 21:7–11; Mk 11:7–10)

3. In 1 and 2 Kings, the king's mother was often mentioned. The queen mother, as she was known, held a position of honor. She was a royal counselor, sat at the king's right hand, and had influence on the king's heart (1 Kings 2:19).
   a) How does this Old Testament position relate to Mary as the Mother of God and man? (Mt 1:20–22; Jn 2:1–5; 19:25–27)
   b) Share your memory of a time when you relied on Mary's intercession. (*CCC* 2679, 2682)

4. Solomon, when given the opportunity to ask for anything he wanted from the Lord, chose ". . . an understanding mind to govern" (1 Kings 3:5–12).
   a) What is another word for "an understanding mind" and what does this word mean? (1 Kings 3:12, 28; also consult the *CCC* glossary)
   b) Why did Solomon ask for this? (1 Kings 3:7–9)
   c) Solomon's gift from the Lord is one of the seven gifts of the Holy Spirit. What are the other six gifts? (*CCC* 1831 and glossary)

5. a) What is the significance of the temple? (1 Kings 5:19; 8:20–21; *CCC* 2580)
   b) What did the temple contain? (1 Kings 8:20–21)
   c) What is the relationship between the temple, Christ, and the Church? (*CCC* 593, 756)

6. It took Solomon seven years to build the temple. With its building, Solomon seemed to have brought David's kingdom to its greatness; how-

ever, his actions then began to weaken it. What laws of God did Solomon disobey? (Deut 17:16–17; 1 Kings 10:14–18, 26–28; 11:3–8)

7. As a result of Solomon's hardness of heart, the Lord revealed that the kingdom would be torn from Solomon's son's hand (1 Kings 11:30–37). Thus, the twelve tribes were divided—ten to the north, called Israel, and two to the south, called Judah. After Solomon, who ruled over Israel? Over Judah? (1 Kings 11:30–31; 12:17, 21)

8. Why were altars for worship built in Bethel and Dan? (1 Kings 12:26–27)

9. Despite their separation, God did not forsake the Northern Kingdom. He sent them Elijah, the prophet. Encountering a widow, Elijah asked her to give him food. List several of the blessings the widow received because of her faith. (1 Kings 17:8–24)

10. Read 1 Kings 18:21–39. The One, True God was evident in response to Elijah's plea: "'Answer me, O LORD, answer me, that this people may know that thou, O LORD, art God, and that thou hast turned their hearts back.' Then the fire of the LORD fell, and consumed the burnt offering, and the wood, and the stones, and the dust, and licked up the water that was in the trench" (1 Kings 18:37–38).
    a) The 450 prophets of Baal were not capable of working against the One, True God. What sign indicated that God accepted the bull offering Elijah had made, and what did this sign symbolize? (CCC 696)
    b) How does this help you understand John the Baptist being referred to as the one who would go before the Lord "in the spirit and power of Elijah" (Lk 1:17)? (CCC 718–19)

11. Like Elijah we also pray that the Lord will hear and answer our prayers, but at times we are uncertain of the answer we receive from God. God, in His faithfulness, shows us, in the prayers of Solomon (1 Kings 8:10–61) and Elijah (1 Kings 18:36–37), examples of sincere and powerful prayer, acknowledging Him as the one and only God.
    a) What is the truth about these examples of prayer? (Jas 5:16b)
    b) A simple way of defining a righteous person might be: one who serves

God through living by faith. As you strive toward righteousness, on what three principal Lukan parables on prayer might you focus to draw closer to God in prayer? (*CCC* 2613)

12. Elisha left all behind to follow Elijah (1 Kings 19:19–21). Jesus made the same demand of His disciples (Mt 4:18–22).
    a) What does it mean for you to leave all and follow Jesus? (Mt 10:37–39; 16:24–25; Lk 9:57–62)
    b) Choose something you need to leave behind to follow Jesus better.

The wrap-up tape segment is 23 minutes, starting at the beginning of Tape 8 and ending at the break, anticipating a discussion with Dr. Hahn and Jeff Cavins.

Note: Please review question 1 of next week's lesson early in the week.

Notes:

Notes:

Chapter Equivalent Reading for Lesson 14: 6¼ chapters

Read 2 Kings 1:1—2:18; 17:1—41; 22:1—23:30; 25:1–30

1. In last week's study, question 12 referred to leaving all and following Jesus. Relate how you were able to incorporate this into your life this week.

2. Part of the blessing, the inheritance, of the first-born was to receive a double portion of his father's property. Although not Elijah's son, Elisha asked for a double portion of his spirit (2 Kings 2:9).
   a) As his inheritance, how was the spirit of Elijah in Elisha? (2 Kings 2:9–15; Lk 1:16–17)
   b) In what way do Christians have a share in that spirit as part of the communion of saints? (*CCC* 960–62, 2683, first half of 2684)
   c) From which saint would you like to request a "double portion"?

3. Read 2 Kings 4:32–37. The woman whose son was restored to life by Elisha expressed gratitude. How can you express gratitude to God? (*CCC* 2638; Lk 17:12–19)

4. Read 2 Kings 4:42–44. Elisha's servant questioned how the bread he had could feed a hundred. How is the Eucharist prefigured here? (Jn 6:12–13, 34–35)

5. The persistent sins of the inhabitants of Israel, the Northern Kingdom, preceded their being taken into exile by the Assyrians (2 Kings 17).
   a) What sins caused the Israelites to be deported? (2 Kings 17:7–25)
   b) How do your sins lead you into "exile"? (*CCC* 1440, first part of 1472)

6. a) How did a devastating national event (seventy years of exile) fit into the Father's eternal plan for Israel? (Ps 138; Is 49:14–17; 55:6–9)
   b) How has or could a devastating personal event (for example, the death of a spouse or child, a job loss, a traumatic illness) fit into the Father's eternal plan for you?

7. During the period of the exile, when they had lost everything, the Israelites had to rely on God alone. How would your life change if you relied on God alone? (*CCC* 301)

8. Josiah, King of Judah, rid the land of the pagan priests, objects, and shrines and restored the observance of the Passover.
   a) What was said concerning Josiah's relationship to the Lord? (2 Kings 23:25)
   b) How are you to be like Josiah in your relationship to the Lord? (*CCC* 2083; Mt 22:36–39)

9. Who captured Jerusalem and destroyed the temple and palace in the Southern Kingdom? (2 Kings 25:1, 21)

10. a) Where was the tribe of Judah taken into exile? (2 Kings 24:14–15; 25:11)
    b) Who was allowed to stay in the land of Judah? (2 Kings 25:12)

The wrap-up tape segment is 28 minutes, beginning with Jeff Cavins and Dr. Hahn discussing prophets. It ends at the conclusion of Tape 8.

Notes:

Notes:

Chapter Equivalent Reading for Lesson 15: 9½ chapters

STUDY QUESTIONS

Read Ezra 1, 3:1—7:6; 9—10 and Nehemiah 3—4, 8—9

1. Recalling last week's lesson, how do you feel about God's dealings with His disobedient children?

2. a) Who allowed God's people, after seventy years in exile, to return to Jerusalem to rebuild the temple? (Ezra 1:1–3)
   b) Who oversaw the beginning of the construction of the temple? (Ezra 3:2, 5:2)

3. Cyrus, king of Persia, conquered Babylon and became its king in 538 B.C. Although considered a pagan, he was used by the Lord to return the people to Jerusalem, declaring the proclamation as given to him by the "LORD, the God of heaven" (Ezra 1:2–3).
   a) How is it that God reveals Himself, even to non-believers? (*CCC* 30, 50)
   b) What is your role in helping others to come to know God? (Mt 28:19–20)

4. When the Israelites returned to Jerusalem from Babylon, they started the rebuilding of the temple. This work was funded by donations from the people. This had also been the case when they built the first sanctuary for the Lord, the tabernacle that was used during the wandering in the desert (Ex 25:1–7).
   a) What is the Church's teaching on tithing? (1 Chron 29:14–17; *CCC* 2041, 2043)
   b) According to the Bible, what is a proper tithe? (Gen 28:22; Heb 7:2,4)

5. All the people gave a great shout of joy as the final foundation stone was laid in the rebuilding of the temple in Jerusalem (Ezra 3:11). There are many comparisons to stones, foundations, and the temple in the Church. Describe *some* of these and how they speak to us as Christians. (1 Cor 3:16; Eph 2:19–22; 1 Tim 3:15b; 1 Pet 2:4–8; *CCC* 756)

6. a) Recall a time when your faith community enthusiastically praised and worshipped God together. (Ezra 3:10–11; *CCC* 2639)
   b) Share information about opportunities to gather in praise and worship.

7. Read Ezra 8:21 and Nehemiah 1:4; 9:1. Fasting is mentioned in both the

Old Testament and the New Testament. Jesus himself fasted, as recorded in Matthew 4:2.

a) What is fasting? (*CCC* glossary)

b) When are we called to fast? (*CCC* 1387, 1438)

c) When have you fasted for spiritual reasons? (*CCC* 1387, 1434) What were the results?

8. Ezra was a scribe versed in the Law of Moses; he worked to restore the Chosen People.

a) How did Ezra deal with the people's transgressions? (Ezra 9:5–9)

b) How did the people themselves deal with their transgressions? (Ezra 10:2–3)

9. Both of the penitential prayers of Ezra (Ezra 9:1–15 and Neh 9:32–37) acknowledged the guilt of the people and sought God's forgiveness. We acknowledge our guilt in the Sacrament of Penance.

a) How do you conduct an examination of conscience? (*CCC* 1454)

b) How might a daily examination of conscience be of use in preparing for the Sacrament of Penance?

10. As cupbearer for King Artaxerxes of Persia, Nehemiah had a prestigious job. Why did he leave that job to go to Jerusalem? (Neh 2:3–5)

11. Ezra prayed before the people, remembering how God had remained faithful—guiding, providing, comforting, strengthening, and forgiving—despite their sinful ways (Neh 9). What two aspects of Christian prayer are evident in Ezra's prayer? (*CCC* 2638–39)

The wrap-up tape segment is 33 minutes, starting at the beginning of Tape 9 and ending at the break with Dr. Hahn.

Notes:

_____

_____

_____

_____

_____

_____

_____

_____

Notes:

Chapter Equivalent Reading for Lesson 16: 17 ¼ chapters

STUDY QUESTIONS

Read 1 Maccabees 1:1—3:26; 4:36–61; 6:1–16; 9:23—16:24

1. What is one thing you learned about prayer last week as we read Ezra's beautiful prayer? (Neh 9:6–37) Consider how you might let this influence your time in prayer.

2. In 1 Maccabees 1:10 we see the installation of King Antiochus, a "sinful root". For two years he plundered the country and desecrated the temple. He then erected a desolating sacrilege, a horrible abomination (1 Mac 1:43–61).
   a) What was this desolating sacrilege? (1 Mac 1:54; 4:41–47; 2 Mac 6:6–11)
   b) What happened to those Israelites who remained true to the Lord? (1 Mac 1:57–63; 2 Mac 6:6–11)

3. While some abandoned the Law, others chose to die rather than profane the holy covenant. (1 Mac 1:62–63a)
   a) How are we called to purity? What are some of the things our society tempts us to do that would be an impurity or abomination?
   b) What virtue will help us in these situations and why? (*CCC* 1808)

4. Who was Mattathias and how many sons did he have? Name them. (1 Mac 2:1–5)

5. a) Read 1 Maccabees 2:34–38, 40–49. Compare how the two groups of Israelites reacted to the same set of circumstances. Which way was the right way to respond? (*CCC* 2306, 2308, 2321)
   b) What are the traditional elements in what is called a "just war" doctrine? (*CCC* 2309)

6. What were the motives behind the Maccabean wars? (1 Mac 3:1–2, 21)

7. After Mattathias died, Judas Maccabeus continued to command Israel's troops.
   a) What gave Judas his victories? (1 Mac 3:18–19, 22)
   b) Share a time when you experienced strength that comes from heaven.

8. What did Judas Maccabeus do after the Israelites' enemies were once more defeated? (1 Mac 4:47–58)

9. Judas Maccabeus died in battle defending the land of Judah. (1 Mac 9:10, 18)
   a) Who succeeded Judas Maccabeus as leader against the Greeks? (1 Mac 9:31)
   b) Simon followed in their footsteps. What did he succeed in doing that his father and brothers could not do? (1 Mac 13:41–42; 2 Mac 14:7, 11–15)

10. With what ruling power did Israel make its final alliance? (1 Mac 15:16–17)

11. As we have studied 1 Maccabees, we have seen how the Israelites surrendered all for their faith; some even gave up their lives. Consider how you might respond to persecution. (*CCC* 1816, 2473)

The wrap-up tape segment is 20 minutes, beginning after the break of last week and ending at the conclusion of Tape 9.

Notes:

Notes:

_____
_____
_____
_____
_____
_____
_____
_____
_____
_____
_____
_____
_____
_____
_____
_____
_____
_____
_____
_____
_____
_____
_____
_____
_____
_____
_____
_____
_____

Chapter Equivalent Reading for Lesson 17: ¾ of a chapter

STUDY QUESTIONS

Read Luke 1:1–4, 26–44; 2:1–7

1. We are crossing the bridge from the Old Testament into the New Testament. What is the relationship between the Old Testament and the New Testament? (*CCC* 128–29, 140)

2. What do we know about the author of Luke's Gospel? (Lk 1:1–4; Col 4:14; 2 Tim 4:9–11; Philem 24)

3. One of the Church's traditional prayers to Mary, the Hail Mary, has two sections—the first section magnifying the Lord for the great things He has done in the life of Mary and the second recognizing Mary's role as intercessor for us (*CCC* 2675).
   a) What are the events that are referred to in the first portion of the Hail Mary? (Lk 1:26–28, 39–42)
   b) What does this prayer teach us about God's and the Church's regard for Mary? (*CCC* 2676–77, 2679)
   c) We sometimes recite memorized prayers quickly, without thought about their content. What phrase of the Hail Mary is particularly meaningful to you?

4. The Rosary consists of three types of mysteries—the Joyful, the Sorrowful, and the Glorious.
   a) The five Joyful Mysteries are all found in Luke. What are they? (Lk 1:26–38, 39–45; 2:1–7, 22–38, 41–51)
   b) What value do you place on the Rosary? (*CCC* 725, 2674, 2708)

5. We have learned that the New Testament lies hidden in the Old and the Old Testament is revealed in the New. For the Israelites the glory of the Lord dwelled in the Ark of the Covenant. The Ark contained the Word of God (the tablets with the Ten Commandments), the "bread" (manna) they were fed, and the rod of Aaron that sprouted miraculously to show that God had called him and his tribe to priestly service. Why is Mary the Ark of the New Covenant? (Jn 1:14; 2:5; 6:49–51; Rev 11:19–12:1, 5. Also compare 2 Sam 6:9 and Lk 1:43; 2 Sam 6:11 and Lk 1:56; 2 Sam 6:14 and Lk 1:44)

6. When the angel Gabriel appeared to Mary, the first words he said were, "Hail, full of grace, the Lord is with you" (Lk 1:28). We see a similar

greeting from an angel in Judges 6:12. The difference between the two exchanges are the words "full of grace", a very unusual form of greeting that the angel Gabriel gave. "The Fathers and Doctors of the Church 'taught that this singular, solemn and unheard-of greeting showed that all the divine graces reposed in the Mother of God and that she was adorned with all the gifts of the Holy Spirit', which meant that she 'was never subject to the curse', that is, was preserved from all sin. These words of the archangel in this text constitute one of the sources which reveal the dogma of Mary's immaculate conception" (cf. Pius IX, *Ineffabilis Deus;* Paul VI, *Creed [Credo] of the People of God,* in *The Navarre Bible: The Gospel of Saint Luke,* p. 37)

    a) What does the Immaculate Conception mean? (*CCC* 487–88, 490–93)

    b) Why was it that Mary, in order to be a proper "ark", needed to be without Original Sin? (Lk 1:28; *CCC* 721–22)

7. In what areas of your life do you find it most difficult to say to God, "Let it be done to me according to your word"? (Lk 1:38)

8. **a)** What was prophesied in Isaiah 7:14, and how was it fulfilled in Luke 1:27?

    b) Jesus is said to be Mary's "first-born son" (Lk 2:7). What meaning did "first-born" have to the Israelites? (Ex 13:1, 11–12a, 14–15)

    c) What is the Church's teaching on Mary's virginity? (*CCC* 499–501)

9. What city was David from? (1 Sam 16:1, 13; Lk 2:4)

The wrap-up tape segment is 32 minutes, starting at the beginning of Tape 10 and ending at the break with Dr. Hahn's invitation to join them in just a minute.

Notes:

_____

_____

_____

_____

_____

_____

_____

Notes:

Chapter Equivalent Reading for Lesson 18: 1¼ chapters

STUDY QUESTIONS

Read Luke 6:20–49; 8:4–18

1. What was something new that you learned last week?

2. What is the meaning of the Incarnation? (*CCC* 461, 464; Lk 2:11; Jn 1:14)

3. **a)** How do you make your Christmas celebrations meaningful?
   b) What is your favorite religious Christmas carol; why does it especially appeal to you?

4. Luke 2:52 reads, "And Jesus increased in wisdom and in stature and in favor with God and man." Various sources have given different erroneous explanations of where and when Jesus "knew" what His mission on earth was. What does the Catholic Church teach on this matter? (Lk 2:40; *CCC* 470–74)

5. In the Sermon on the Plain, Jesus gave us the Beatitudes (Lk 6:20–26; see also the Sermon on the Mount, Mt 5:1–12). Why are they important to us? (*CCC* 1716–19, 1728, and glossary)

6. Read Luke 6:20, 24; 16:19–25; 18:25. In Matthew 5:3 we are given a fuller explanation of the meaning of the virtue of poverty. "As early as St Augustine's time there were people who failed to understand poverty and riches properly; they reasoned as follows: The Kingdom of heaven belongs to the poor, the Lazaruses of this world, the hungry; all the rich are bad, like this rich man here. This sort of thinking led St Augustine to explain . . . 'Do not despise rich men who are merciful, who are humble: or, to put it briefly, do not despise poor rich men. Oh, poor man!, be poor yourself; poor, that is, humble . . . and remember that Abraham was a very wealthy man when he was on earth: he had abundance of money, a large family, flocks, land; yet that rich man was poor, because he was humble' (*Sermon* 14)" (quoted in the *Navarre Bible: The Gospel of Saint Luke*, pp. 97–98). To tie this all together, poverty not only refers to that which is external, but is also something that refers to the disposition of a person's heart and soul.
   a) Explain how it is possible to be a "poor rich man". (*CCC* 1351, 2559)
   b) How were Abraham, Isaac, Moses, David, and Job "poor rich men"?

(Gen 14:18–24; 22:15–17; Ex 3:11; 15:2–3; Job 1:1–3, 8, 20–21; Ps 131:1–2)

7. Luke 6:27–49 can be summarized by listing four spiritual practices that are meant to be a part of every Christian's life:
   a) Live by the Golden Rule, Luke 6:27–36.
   b) Recognize your own faults, Luke 6:37–42.
   c) Have a good heart, Luke 6:43–45.
   d) Base your life on the Rock, Luke 6:46–49.
   (*Commentary on the Gospel of Luke,* A. McBride, pp. 67–68)
   Select one of these and share how you put it into practice in your own walk with the Lord.

8. In the Parable of the Sower (Lk 8:4–8), the seed fell on different types of soil.
   a) Name the different types of soil.
   b) Explain the Parable of the Sower. (Lk 8:11–15)

9. Consider the four types of soil in the Parable of the Sower. Share times in your life when you have had different types of soil for receiving the seed.

10. a) Parables were a characteristic method used by Jesus for teaching. Why did Jesus speak in parables? (*CCC* 546 and glossary; Mt 13:13–17)
    b) Why did some not understand His parables? (Mt 11:25–27; 13:13–17; *CCC* 544)

The wrap-up tape segment is 21 minutes, beginning after the break from lesson 17 and ending with the conclusion of Tape 10.

Notes:

_____

_____

_____

_____

_____

_____

Notes:

Chapter Equivalent Reading for Lesson 19: 2¾ chapters

STUDY QUESTIONS

Read Luke 17:11; 22:7—23:49

1. What from last week's study was most meaningful to you?

2. During his public life Jesus had traveled to Jerusalem two previous times. Why was this journey (Lk 17:11; 19:28) of particular significance? (*CCC* 557; Lk 9:51; Jn 13:1)

3. After the third temptation in the desert (Lk 4:13), the devil departed from Jesus until an opportune time. How is Satan evident in the events surrounding Christ's Passion? (Lk 22:3–6, 31–32, 60–62)

4. The Passover was a solemn occasion commemorating the deliverance of the Israelites from Egypt at the time of Moses and their covenant relationship with God. How does the lamb of the Passover prefigure Christ, the Paschal Lamb? (Ex 12:3–14; *CCC* 608)

5. At the Last Supper, Our Lord changed bread and wine into His Body and Blood, thereby instituting the Sacrament of the Eucharist.
   a) Eucharist means "thanksgiving". For what are we giving thanks? (*CCC* 1328, 1360)
   b) How might you explain to others that the Eucharist is the Real Presence of Jesus' Body, Blood, soul, and divinity? (Jn 6:52–69; 1 Cor 11:23–29; *CCC* 1374)

6. What do we call the change that takes place in the bread and wine at the Consecration, and what does this mean? (*CCC* 1376)

7. Share feelings and thoughts you have had in receiving Christ in the Eucharist.

8. Luke tells us that it was Jesus' custom to go to the Mount of Olives to pray (Lk 22:39). The action of the Holy Spirit and the importance of prayer in Jesus' ministry are emphasized in the fact that He prayed before the decisive moments of His mission, humbly committing His human will to His Father's will (*CCC* 2600). If we are to be imitators of Christ, we must have a desire to be strengthened in our commitment to the Father's will. This presupposes we have a desire to know the Father's will—a knowledge that comes from time spent in prayer.

a) Although we know the necessity of prayer in the growth of Christian life, why is it difficult to have a prayer life? (*CCC* 2725–28)

b) As we have addressed prayer during this study, how have you been able to respond to your difficulties with prayer?

9. Luke carefully narrates the story of our Lord's Passion to emphasize the forgiveness of sin. While Jesus was being beaten and ridiculed, Peter three times denied knowing him (Lk 22:56–65). Earlier, Christ had revealed Peter's weakness to him (Lk 22:31–32), telling him that He had prayed that Peter's faith would not fail and that once he turned back, he would strengthen his brothers. Thereafter, having been scourged, crowned with thorns, spat upon, made to carry the cross, stripped of His clothes, nailed to the cross and approaching death, Jesus took what little strength He had left to pray for forgiveness for those who had taken part in His Passion (Lk 23:34). After Christ's Resurrection, Peter reconciled with Christ, and his friendship with Him was renewed (Jn 21:15–17). As Christians, by our thoughts, words, and deeds, we sometimes deny knowing Christ. How can we see and experience in the Sacrament of Penance the same effects of forgiveness Peter experienced? (*CCC* 1422, 1468–69)

10. As Christ carried the cross to Calvary, He grew weary. Simon from Cyrene was made to shoulder the cross (Lk 23:26).
    a) Why do you think Luke states that Simon walked *behind* Jesus? (Lk 9:23; 14:27)
    b) When have you shouldered another's burdens, perhaps with a prompting from the Holy Spirit?

11. Jesus' redemptive death on the cross immediately drew people to Him.
    a) What was the effect of Jesus' Passion and death on those people who encountered Him at the cross? (Lk 23:39–43, 47–48; Mt 27:54)
    b) How was this foretold by Jesus and extended to all? (Jn 12:32; *CCC* 542)

The wrap-up tape segment is 34 minutes, starting at the beginning of Tape 11 and ending at the break reminder that they'll return in just a minute.

Notes:

_____

_____

_____

_____

Notes:

Chapter Equivalent Reading for Lesson 20: 1 chapter

Read Luke 24

1. **a)** Reflecting on last week's study, what portion of the Passion touches you most deeply?
   b) In light of what you have read, do you think crucifixes truly reflect Christ's suffering? Why or why not?

2. On the first day of the week, the women went with spices to prepare Christ's body, only to find the tomb empty.
   a) What is the importance of this event happening on the first day of the week? (Lk 24:1; Acts 20:7; *CCC* 2174)
   b) Why did Sunday replace the Sabbath (for Jews, Saturday) as the day of worship? (Lk 24:1; *CCC* 1193, 2175, 2190–91)

3. Why is the Resurrection of Jesus (Lk 24:1–9) the cornerstone of our faith? (1 Cor 15:12–19; *CCC* 638, 642, 651–55)

4. Doubt again surfaced in the disciples. The story told by the women who had found the empty tomb seemed like nonsense and was not believed by the Eleven (Lk 24:11). Peter went home after seeing the empty tomb, amazed at what he had seen (Lk 24:12). Thomas refused to believe unless he saw and touched the nail marks in Christ's hands and feet and put his hand into His side (Jn 20:25). And even just before the Ascension of Jesus, at the commissioning of the disciples, some continued to doubt (Mt 28:17).
   a) How does the presence of this doubt in the disciples help reinforce the Church's teaching on the Resurrection of Christ? (*CCC* 643–44)
   b) When you experience doubt, how should you understand and overcome it? (*CCC* 157, 2088; Mk 9:23–24)

5. How was Christ's Resurrection different from the raisings from the dead that Jesus had performed during His earthly ministry? (*CCC* 645–46)

6. On the road to Emmaus, the men did not recognize Jesus as they left Jerusalem (Lk 24:13–18), nor did the apostles know Him when He first appeared to them. The apostles thought they were seeing a ghost (Lk 24:36–37).
   a) What did Jesus do to open the eyes of those He encountered after His Resurrection? (Lk 24:30–31, 39, 42–43)
   b) Share a time when He has opened your eyes.

7. Just as Jerusalem was the completion of Christ's journey, it was the beginning of His disciples' journeys.
   a) How did Christ prepare His disciples? (Lk 24:44–52)
   b) What did He ask of them? (Mt 28:19–20; Acts 1:8)

8. Share a time when your openness to the Scriptures enabled you to witness to the truth of Christ.

9. What is the Ascension? (*CCC* 659, 665, glossary)

The wrap-up tape segment is 20 minutes, beginning after the break of the previous week and ending at the conclusion of Tape 11.

Notes:

Notes:

Chapter Equivalent Reading for Lesson 21: 1 chapter

STUDY QUESTIONS

Read Acts 1:1—2:13

1. How do the events of Christ's life, death, and Resurrection fulfill Our Father's Plan?

2. Who wrote Acts of the Apostles? (Acts 1:1; Lk 1:3)

3. a) What were the criteria for naming Judas Iscariot's replacement? (Acts 1:21–22)
   b) Why was it important to have Judas' position as an apostle filled by another, keeping the number to twelve? (Mt 19:28; Lk 22:29–30; *CCC* 551, 765)

4. As the Father guided the Israelites throughout salvation history, bringing it to a culmination in the fulfillment of His plan in Christ, so He continues to guide our living in Christ through the Church. Acts 1:15–26 gives the account of Peter, as head of the Church, leading the apostles, as the bishops, in the selection of Judas' successor. What are the Pope's and the bishops' relationship and responsibilities in leading the Church? (*CCC* 880–85)

5. Acts might have been called the "Gospel of the Holy Spirit". On several occasions Jesus promised to send the Holy Spirit, and in Acts we see how the Holy Spirit guided the beginnings of the Church. Read John 7:39; 16:7–15; Acts 1:2, 4–5; 2:33.
   a) Why is Pentecost celebrated as the birth of Christ's Church? (*CCC* 729–30, 732, 737–38, 1076)
   b) When is Pentecost celebrated? (*CCC* 731)

6. What three outward signs or symbols accompanied the descent of the Holy Spirit at Pentecost? (Acts 2:1–4)

7. Those gathered together on Pentecost received the fulfillment of Jesus' promise that they would receive power from the Holy Spirit coming upon them (Acts 1:8; 2:1–4).
   a) How is this power of the Holy Spirit, completing our initiation into the Church, given to Catholics today? (*CCC* 1288)
   b) What are the effects of this Sacrament? (*CCC* 1303, 1316)

8. **a)** What are the gifts of the Holy Spirit? (*CCC* 1831 and glossary)
   b) What are the fruits of the Holy Spirit? (*CCC* 1832 and glossary)
   c) What is the relationship between the gifts and the fruits of the Holy Spirit? (*CCC* 1830–32)
   d) Ask someone close to you which fruit(s) he sees most evident in your life.

9. What is your Confirmation name? Why did you choose it?

10. Gathered in Jerusalem for the Pentecost festival were Jews from every nation (Acts 2:5). After being filled with the Holy Spirit, the apostles were able to begin the mission given to them by Jesus before His Ascension, that of declaring the Good News to all nations and baptizing in the name of the Father and the Son and the Holy Spirit (Mt 28:19–20).
   a) What is the Church's teaching today concerning our missionary work? (*CCC* 851, 854–56)
   b) In what ways have you been a missionary in today's world? (Consider your home, workplace, Church, neighborhood, and so forth)

The wrap-up tape segment is 32 minutes. It starts at the beginning of Tape 12 and ends with the mention of the upcoming discussion about *sola scriptura* and *sola fide,* leading to the break.

Notes:

Notes:

Chapter Equivalent Reading for Lesson 22: 2¾ chapters

STUDY QUESTIONS

Read Acts 9:1—11:19

1. From last week's questions and video, what do you find most intriguing about the beginnings of the Church?

2. On the road to Damascus, Saul encountered the Risen Christ in a powerful way.
   a) What was Saul's plan on his way to Damascus? (Acts 9:1–2)
   b) How does Christ's answer to Saul's question, "Who are you, Lord?" (Acts 9:4–5), apply to us today? (Mt 25:45; Heb 6:6; *CCC* 598)

3. a) How did the Jews and the early Christians treat Saul, and why? (Acts 9:13–14, 21, 23, 26, 29)
   b) Describe a situation where you have wrestled with discerning the validity of another's preaching (for example, radio and television evangelists, cults, friends).

4. What did Cornelius and Peter each do before he experienced his vision that showed he was honestly seeking God? (Acts 10:2, 9)

5. Acts 10:1–48 tells of Cornelius, who was not a Jew but a Roman centurion. Up to this time the Gospel had been preached only to the Jews and the Samaritans (who had originally been part of the Chosen People). In Matthew 10:6 Jesus instructed His disciples to preach "to the lost sheep of the house of Israel". God now took steps to reveal a new truth to Peter. What is the new truth God wanted to reveal to Peter? (*CCC* 851; Acts 10:34; 11:18; Rom 2:11; Eph 6:9)

6. In Acts 10 Peter came to realize God's plan for His Church, but it was not without some hesitation. Whom do you find hard to accept as being called by God?

7. Describe the circumstances surrounding the first non-Jewish Baptism. (Acts 10:44–48)

8. Baptism is evident in the early Church, and it had been commanded by Christ in the Great Commission (Mt 28:19–20).
   a) What significance do you see in the Baptisms mentioned in this week's readings (Acts 10, about Cornelius, and Acts 11, about the Gentiles in general)?

b) What is the Church's teaching concerning the necessity of Baptism for salvation? (*CCC* 1226, 1257–61)

9. Tradition regards Saint Stephen as the first Christian martyr (Acts 7:59–60; 11:19).
   a) What is a martyr? (*CCC* 852, 2473; Acts 22:20; Rev 17:6)
   b) What cardinal virtue helps those faced with martyrdom? (*CCC* 1808)
   c) How can we, today, benefit from the saints and martyrs? (*CCC* 828, 1173)

The wrap-up tape segment is 19 minutes, starting with Dr. Hahn and Jeff Cavins discussing *sola scriptura* and *sola fide* and ending at the conclusion of Tape 12.

Notes:

Notes:

Chapter Equivalent Reading for Lesson 23: 6 chapters

STUDY QUESTIONS

Read Acts 13:1—18:22

1. Last week we learned of the Church reaching out to the Gentiles and the uncircumcised. How does the awareness that God continually seeks all people to be united with Him affect your view of God?

2. The first twelve chapters of Acts show how Peter and the disciples were involved in spreading the Good News throughout Jerusalem, Judea, and Samaria. The Church continued to grow throughout the time recorded in Acts, reaching more distant lands.
   a) From what city was the new missionary activity initiated? (Acts 13:1–3)
   b) Who joined Barnabas and Saul on their first mission to proclaim the Word of God on Cyprus? (Acts 12:12, 25; 13:5)

3. Paul's first preaching is sometimes referred to as his inaugural address (Acts 13:17–39). In this discourse, Paul reviewed the Old Testament events that led to the lineage of Jesus and how He fulfilled the Scriptures in His death and Resurrection. How is Paul's address in the synagogue similar to Peter's speeches at Pentecost (Acts 2:22–32) and at Solomon's Portico (Acts 3:13–15)?

4. Throughout his missionary journey, Paul encountered persecution and hardship. He reminded the new Christians that they too would face hardships, but he reassured them that there would be elders (Acts 20:17–32) to help them. These special men helped the early Christian communities grow by sharing the Word of God and the Sacraments. In the New Testament, a man becomes a priest through a special calling from God.
   a) What is the Sacrament of Holy Orders? (*CCC* 1536)
   b) Why is the Sacrament called "Orders"? (*CCC* 1537–38)
   c) In what priestly function do priests "exercise in a supreme degree their sacred office," and why? (*CCC* 1566)

5. a) Barnabas and Paul returned to Antioch after a successful mission. Upon their return, they found a debate taking place because some Judeans were teaching that circumcision was necessary for salvation. In an attempt to resolve this dilemma, the Council of Jerusalem was held. What answer did Peter provide? (Acts 15:1–2, 6–11)

b) Since the Council of Jerusalem, there have been many councils and synods, including Ecumenical Councils. An Ecumenical Council is a gathering of all the world's bishops, usually called by the Pope, not to make new doctrine but to reinforce and clarify Church teaching. How many Ecumenical Councils have taken place during the Church's history? What is the most recent one? (See "Ecumenical Councils" in the *CCC* index of citations.)

6. Peter, having been given the keys to the kingdom as head of the Church, demonstrated his leadership at Jerusalem. What is the foundation of the Church's teaching concerning the Pope's leadership? (Is 22:22–24; Mt 16:16–19; Rev 3:7; *CCC* 880–81)

7. As successor to Peter, today's Pope can also speak with authority on behalf of the Church. What is this authority called, and when is the Pope speaking in this manner? (*CCC* 889, 891)

8. There were many instances of disagreement in the young Church. We are no different today. When you have a misunderstanding or conflict with another, how should it be resolved? (Mt 5:23–25; 18:15–17; Rom 14:10–13; Eph 4:1–3; Col 3:8–15)

9. Paul and his companions were seeking a "place of prayer" on the Sabbath (Acts 16:13).
    a) Consider your travels. Reflect on your efforts to find a place to join in the Mass. What have been your experiences?
    b) Where is your personal place of prayer at home? (*CCC* 2691, 2757; Mk 1:35; Lk 5:16)

10. The Catholic Church, unlike many Protestant religions, encourages infant Baptism. Why do we baptize infants? (Gen 17:9–12; Lk 2:21–22; Acts 16:14–15, 33–34; *CCC* 403, 1250–52)

The wrap-up tape segment is 34 minutes, starting at the beginning of Tape 13 and ending at the break during the discussion of the book of Revelation.

Notes:

_____

_____

_____

_____

_____

Notes:

Chapter Equivalent Reading for Lesson 24: 3 chapters

STUDY QUESTIONS

Read Acts 18:18—21:16

1. How has the study of *Our Father's Plan* affected your spiritual growth?

2. Apollos was an eloquent speaker and an authority on Scripture, but he lacked instruction in "the Way" (Acts 18:24–26). What does it mean to say that Christianity is "the Way"? (Jn 14:6)

3. The book of Acts shows the importance the early Church placed on teaching "the Way", of clarifying what was necessary, expected, and helpful in following Jesus. The Church today continues to provide guidance and disciplines to promote growth in our faith life.
   a) What are the Precepts of the Church? (*CCC* 2041–43)
   b) How can each guide the growth of our faith?

4. What is the difference between the baptism of John the Baptist and that of the apostles after Christ's Resurrection? (Acts 1:5; 19:1–6)

5. a) Ephesus was a town where a large number of silversmiths resided. Why were the townspeople roused with anger at the speech given by the silversmith named Demetrius? (Acts 19:23–27)
   b) What did Paul do? (Acts 19:30–31; 20:1)

6. Paul stated that the importance of his life was his faithfulness, his finishing the course, and the ministry he received from Jesus (Acts 20:24). Some Christians believe salvation is a one-time act: "Once saved, always saved". What is the Church's teaching concerning the necessity of "persevering in faith to the end"? (Mt 10:22; Lk 8:11–15; 1 Cor 9:27; 1 Tim 1:18–19; 2 Tim 2:12; *CCC* 161–62)

7. How would you describe Paul's role in Our Father's Plan? (Acts 9:1–21; 20:18–24; Rom 1:1; Gal 1:11–24; 1 Thess 2:2–12)

8. When have you used the phrase found in Acts 21:14? What does it mean to you? (*CCC* 2059)

9. It was a real struggle for Jewish Christians to accept Gentiles into the faith. What would make you feel more welcomed in your parish family?

10. The book of Acts covers a time of approximately thirty years, beginning with Christ's Ascension and the birth of the Catholic Church and ending with Paul's captivity in Rome (A.D. 61–63). These years saw incredible missionary work and the spread of Christianity. In the New Testament, there are many letters of encouragement, instruction, and correction that were written to the newly formed Christian communities. How are the Acts of the Apostles and many of these letters related? Compare:

a) Acts 9:24–25 and 2 Cor 11:32–33

b) Acts 14:1, 5–6, 19–20 and 2 Tim 3:10–11

c) Acts 16:6 and Gal 1:1–2, 6

d) Acts 16:12 and Phil 1:1–3

e) Acts 17:1–2 and 1 Thess 1:1–5

f) Acts 18:2 and Rom 1:1, 7, 13–14

g) Acts 19:1 and Eph 1:1–2

h) Acts 28:16 and Phil 1:13–14; 2 Tim 1:16–17

The wrap-up tape segment is 20 minutes, starting with the discussion of the anti-Christ and the rapture and ending with the conclusion of the tape.

Notes:

Notes:

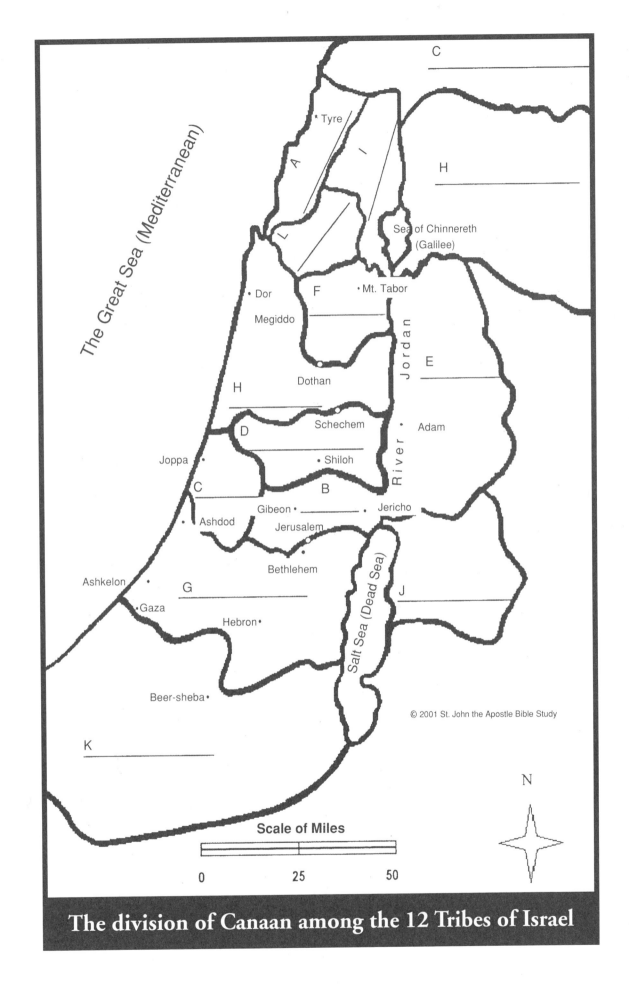

The division of Canaan among the 12 Tribes of Israel

BIBLIOGRAPHY

1. Alexander, David, and Pat Alexander, eds. *Eerdmans Handbook to the Bible*. Grand Rapids, Mich.: Wm. B. Eerdmans Publishing Co., 1992.

2. Baker, Kenneth, S.J. *Inside the Bible*. San Francisco: Ignatius Press, 1998.

3. *Catechism of the Catholic Church*. Second edition. Vatican City: Libreria Editrice Vaticana, and Washington, D.C.: United States Catholic Conference, 1994, 1997.

4. *Every Catholic's Guide to the Sacred Scriptures*. Nashville: Thomas Nelson Publishers, 1990.

5. Faculty of Theology of the University of Navarre. *The Navarre Bible: The Gospel of Saint Luke*. Dublin: Four Courts Press, 1988.

6. Faculty of Theology of the University of Navarre. *The Navarre Bible: The Pentateuch*. Dublin: Four Courts Press, and Princeton: Scepter Publishers, 1999.

7. Leon-Dufour, Xavier, ed. *Dictionary of Biblical Theology*. Boston: St. Paul Books and Media, 1995.

8. McBride, Alfred, O.P. *Commentary on the Gospel of Luke*. Huntington, Ind.: OSV Publishing, 1992.

9. Paul VI. *Credo of the People of God*, June 30, 1968.

10. Pius IX. *Ineffabilis Deus*, December 8, 1954.

Notes:

Notes:

Notes:

Notes: